Sour(

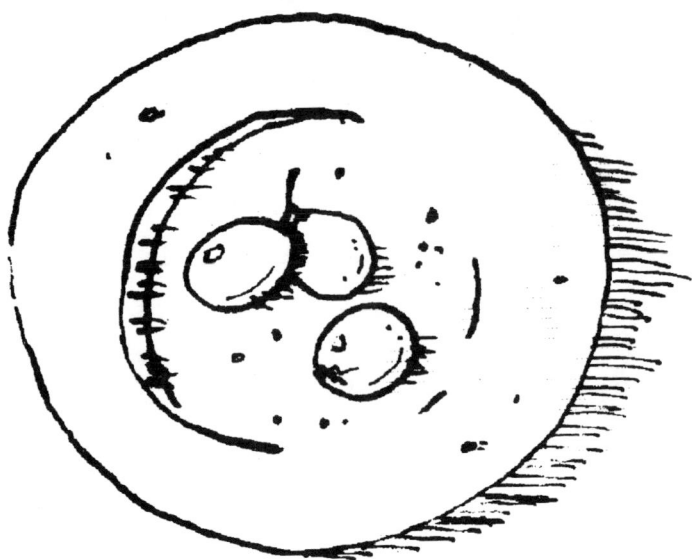

Sour Grapes

ribald rhymes by

Clive Murphy

illustrated by

Gary Parkinson

the bad press

Published in 1999 by The Bad Press,
PO Box 76, Manchester M21 8HJ
www.thebadpress.com

ISBN 0 9517233 9 1

1 3 5 7 9 2 4 6 8

Cover designed by Gary Parkinson.

Printed by
The Arc and Throstle Press Limited,
Nanholme Mill, Shaw Wood Road,
Todmorden, Lancs, OL14 6DA.

Distributed by
Turnaround Ltd,
27 Horsell Road,
London, N5 1XL.

Contents

for
P D

Variation on an Old Choosing Rhyme

AC/DC mainie mo
Catch a bugger by the toe
If he hollers let him go
AC/DC quid pro quo
You - are - Shit

Untrammelled Pleasure

Oh, what a beautiful mornin'
Oh, what a beautiful gay -
I got a beautiful feelin'
He's not goin' to ask me to pay.

Betrayal

"May I introduce my wife?"
"Oh, you mean your 'other life'?"

Memory of The Rockingham

Poofs with hard faces
Giving themselves airs and graces.

Self-Timer

Let's snap each other in cahoots
And send the film elsewhere than Boots'.

Volta-faccia

Georgie Porgie, pudding and pie,
Kissed his wife and made her cry.
When the boys came out to play
George and Gilbert ran away.

Impressed Youth to a 'Name' in Debrett

History seeps from your very balls.
I am not worthy to wash your smalls.

Water Sports

"Forgive the colour of my pee.
Vitamin B."

'Fifteen Acorns Are Hardly Worth the Price of Admission' (After reading Noel Coward's comment on a casting of David Storey's play 'The Changing Room')

Has-been,
Size queen,
Silly bugger!
League Table
Doesn't mean
Hung like Burgess, Gable...
It's prowess at rugger!

On Drag Queens Who Mime
to the Voice of Shirley Bassey

I understand it
But I can't stand it.

Correct Pronunciation or
Cinema Disappointment
(for Joy Puritz)

What your mack's hid
Is flaccid.

Holiday

Not cruising. Coasting.
No fly-posting.

A Virgin Speaks

Stop Complaining.
This is On The Job Training.

Party Postmortem, London SW6

So I shouldn't have ought
Tell your guests I hate sport.
To 'adore' powder blue
Also gave them a clue.
And Proust or some highbrow
Would not raise an eyebrow,
But need I have said
I take *Zipper* to bed?

No, I *will* not wash up,
Help to put your flat right
And, after, canoodle
The rest of the night.
I prefer powder blue
And you've made me see red.
I'll return to E2 to read *Zipper* instead.

No Question

"Would you know I was gay?"
"*I'll* say!"

At a Gathering of Intellectuals

"Never 'eard of Levi Strauss.
Want a blow-job on the 'ouse?" -
The wisest words boy ever uttered:
He knew which side his bread was buttered.

Mutual Masturbation

Poets polishing
Critics demolishing.

Cattiness

You say my cats have fleas.
Better than having *your* disease!

One Risk Too Many

He asked him not to use a sheath.
Another wreath.

Failed Candidates #1

I'd assign you my fantasy
shares in the Ritz
If you didn't have safety-pins
stuck through your tits.

Failed Candidates #2

I like your willie.
It's you that's silly.

Failed Candidates #3

A fruit would suit -
But a lush to boot!!?

Failed candidates #4

Your looks are spiffy
But you smell like the Liffey.

Failed Candidates #5

Your mind's impressive.
Your cock's excessive.

Failed Candidates #6
(To one of the cloth)

I'd let you in
But you think it's a sin.

Shameless Blarney

"Yes, I'd a pash
For Ogden Nash,
And Wendy Cope
Once gave me hope.
But - I blush a bit
To mention it -
Who's turned me on
The most is Bron*."

*Mr Auberon Waugh, crusader for poetry
that rhymes, scans and makes sense

After Discovering Dingleberries

Hop it
Or you'll cop it.

**For God's Sake Hold Thy Tongue
And Let Me Love!**

Don't *prattle*!
I can't do battle.

Rape at Tea-Time on a Wet Day

The pot's protrusion
Brings disillusion.
Only humour remains.
You pour within:
Outside it rains.

The Ungracious Guest

So you don't admire my pitch,
You finicking he-bitch!
Next time, if there's a next time and I've energy,
I'll deck my rooms with Koons
and ill-rhymed Fabergé.
That should make those
squeamish 'taste' buds *really* twitch!

SM

"Of course I haven't had enough!
Can't you see I like it rough?!
Dash me to the floor and bash me!
Lash me to the door and thrash me!
Then go through the drill again
With manacles and ball and chain!"

My God, he sees no irony here.
He's getting out the bally gear
And looking earnest and imperious
As if I had been deadly serious.
Will he shatter me limb by limb
If I ask would it matter if I bully him?

I'm working hard. I feel quite sick
But turning the tables did the trick.
I always make the same old bloomer -
Fail to check they've a sense of humour.

Fag Hag

Embodiment of loneliness sublime
In, yet out of, Pantomime.

Literary Conundrum

Could Stein have loved Toklas
If Alice weren't cockless?

A Wit to Someone His Junior

Kiss me, honey, Bosie child.
I'm feeling Oscular and Wilde.

Ex-Offender in Club Backroom on his First Night of Freedom

"In jail,"
He mused with a nostalgic frown,
"I got my tail
In comfort, lying down."

Indifferent Cooking

That's not scrambled egg, Ma.
It's smegma.

Haiku #1

Fun millinery,
Rings and embroidered dresses
For greyscene bishops.

Haiku #2

Opera programmes.
Twittering Humpty Dumpties
Using them as fans.

Haiku #1

Highlights, slap, cheap scent.
The National Film Theatre.
Judy Garland buffs.

Haiku #2

Opera programmes.
Twittering Humpty Dumpties
Using them as fans.

Haiku #3

Highlights, slap, cheap scent.
The National Film Theatre.
Judy Garland buffs.

Haiku #4

Gurgling urinals.
Roundheads, Cavaliers ensnared
By Pretty Police.

A Masochist Compliments His Masseur at a Health Club

"It hurt me greatly. Thanks a lot,
You Kampuchean, you Son of Pol Pot,
You ex-Khmers Rouges
From the slums of Phnom Penh.
Here's fifty quid. Please start again.
Let my back be those fields. I'm perfectly willing.
Stamp even harder. Pretend that you're killing."

A Practised Seducer Meets His Too Sober Match

"Relax, baby!"
"Maybe
Some other night
When I'm not *up*tight
But tight."

Gossip About an Oldie

"He no longer gives satisfaction.
Retraction."

Interruption

"There isn't a doubt, look you.
Good breeding shows:
My Morgan got over his lavender pose.
Yours wasn't a pose, Dai.
Be honest, Dai, do!
You're a hundred percenter:
You're gay through and through.
Stop phoning poor Morgan right out of the blue.
We were just getting down to a bloody good
screw.

You've been holding him back,
you perv forty-niner;
He'd now be with Railtrack instead of a miner.
We've only two kids and a beat-up old Honda;
But for you we'd have four and an A.M. Lagonda,
And I'm sure at the pithead
His mind wouldn't wander
If you didn't keep ringing Porthcawl
from the Rhondda.

You're bent and you're ruining his life and mine.
We're fucking, I told you, Dai. Get off the line!"

Unrequited Love

She fell, poor dear, in love with Ted,
Although she didn't know,
And ev'ry time he wrote more verse,
She said, "It's worse than *Crow!*"

She stayed, poor dear, in love with Ted,
Although she didn't twig,
And, when he wrote of Royalty,
Said, "Hypocrite and prig!"

Today, poor dear, she read of Ted
That she'd be ever free.
She wept onto my answerphone,
"He's gorn at last. Yippee!"

Honest Children's Home Worker to His Partner

You'll be sole breadwinner for a while.
I've told the boss I'm a paedophile.

An Irishman's Loss of Faith

I slept contented,
Now I'm demented.
To call me adorable
Was deplorable:
To take my purse
Was even worse.

I gave my trust. You slaked your lust,
Then stole from me. Me heart is bust.
You were the man I pinned some hope on.
Henceforth I'll sleep with one eye open.
How dare you have your cake and eat it!
I'm in despair 'cause doubly cheated.

Inspired Explanation to Detective for Lingering in a Public Lavatory

It's not what you think, mate.
Enlarged prostate.

Applause

Clap, clap,
I walk with echoing tread.
The early streets are mine.
Clap, clap,
Old chap, it's cleared my head,
This frosty anodyne.
Clap, clap,
You thought yourself so fine
When I shared your tousled bed.
Clap, clap,
For what was hideous is dead.